THE LITHIUM CHRONICLES

VOLUME ONE

NICOLE LYONS

INDIE BLU(E)
PUBLISHING

PRAISE FOR THE LITHIUM CHRONICLES

"If we ever needed a poet laureate of brave, broken, real people who survive the darkness, Nicole Lyons would get my vote, as she is my queen of hearts. She's a heart breaker, a heart mender, a best friend, a warrior, a solace, a rage against the dying light and a new element in the natural world that they haven't yet named. Hell, I'm fairly sure she makes the sun shine and thunder roar. Such is her own, wild, untamed and brilliant voice." - Candice Daquin, author of **A Jar For The Jarring**

"Nicole Lyons is one of the most exciting, vital poets of our generation. **The Lithium Chronicles** *is her most ambitious and brazen work to date, and she delivers above and beyond. Nicole's ability to delve deep into the human psyche, unapologetic, is her gift to the world. Penning a full range of raw, honest, rage and brutal emotion in six lines is her mastery and magic."* - Jacqueline Cioffa, Mental Health Advocate and author of **The Vast Landscape, Georgia Pine**, and **The Red Bench**

"Nicole Lyons has a beautiful treasure chest of poems in **The Lithium Chronicles***, a magical kingdom of deep and powerful words where it's not always sunshine but You'll love her thunder and rain."* - Matthew Spenser, author of **From The Ashes**

The Lithium Chronicles Volume One
Copyright © 2019 by Nicole Lyons.

ISBN: 978-1-7328000-4-5
Library of Congress Control Number: 2019938009

Editors: Christine E. Ray and Kindra M Austin
Cover Design: Mitch Green
Typesetting & Layout: Mitch Green

DEDICATION

For my mother, the creator of my heart and the ache in my head, who demanded excellence but always recognized goodness even when she, and her life, was anything but.

For my mother, the love in my soul and the hope in my heart, and for all the rest of us who have learned to ache like she has.

For my mother, who always dimmed her own light so mine could shine.

I love you.

I love you beyond words and heartbeats, beyond graves and memories, I love you.

NICOLE LYONS

TABLE OF CONTENTS

15   NOT ENTIRELY BROKEN, NEVER QUITE WHOLE

16   IN ALL THAT I AM

17   THE DRAW

18   MY DAYS ARE NUMBERED

19   A DEVIL AND A DEITY

20   IMPETUS

21   BLOOD MOON

22   THEY TAKE ME UNDER, SOMETIMES

23   OF MANIACS AND MANICS

24   SOMETHING PURE

25   FREIGHT TRAINS

26   AN EARWORM IN A GHOST

27   STEALING BREATH

28   DEPRESSION SLEEPS

29   ANOTHER SEASON

30   THE LONG ROAD HOME

31   MELANCHOLY

32   A COLLECTION OF MADNESS AND MAGIC

33   MIDNIGHT MIND

34   MY MANIC MIND

37   A POCKET FULL OF MANIA

38   FAST AND FEROCIOUS

39   A FURIOUS ASCENSION

40   BENEATH DARKNESS

41   EERIE ALONES AND JAMS OF TRAFFIC

42   SHADES OF NEVER ENOUGH

43   WHEN MY SHADOW SPEAKS

44   I HAVE SURRENDERED ON THIS NIGHT

45   ANCHORED

46   THIS SIDE OF MIDNIGHT

47   I SEE YOU

48   MESSY SHINE

49   FROM STEADY SHORES

50   SHE IS A STORM
51   SHE WAS
52   O NEGATIVE
53   FEEDING TIME
54   PERCUSSION
55   THE COSMOS ARE IN A GODDESS
56   CALL ME A GODDESS AGAIN
57   MIXED WITH A HINT
58   LONGING
59   UNDER RED SKIES
60   ON THE HIPS OF A HURRICANE
61   STAR SONGS AND MOONLIGHT
62   STICKY SOUR DANCING
63   BUT YOU WERE
64   ILLUSIONS OF LOVE
65   NEITHER HEAVEN NOR HELL
66   I SHOULD HAVE KNOWN BETTER
67   SOMETHING ACHINGLY BEAUTIFUL
68   JUNK
69   HEAVY HANDS
70   PEACE BY PIECE
71   THE NIGHT A BLUE MOON BURST
72   EVANESCENCE
73   THE COLOUR OF US
74   A COSMIC DISAPPOINTMENT
75   SINISTER LOVERS
76   TOMB GRAZING
77   THE SILENCE OF YOU
78   LITTLE DEATHS
79   TASTING PAIN
80   FUCK YOU, DARLING
81   TO NOTHING
82   MY EASY HEART
83   CAN'T HAVE IT ALL

84	GLEAMING BONES
85	THE OFFERING
86	SACRIFICE
87	JUST YOU WAIT
88	LITTLE BLACK DRESS
89	I ONCE WAS NEW
90	I COULD ALMOST SPARKLE
91	DISCHARGED
92	I WAS HERE
93	LOVE HAS NEVER
94	STOIC
95	BURSTING PURE AND BLOOMING
96	HUSH
97	THAT DAY, AT DINNER
98	GUTTING THE APARTMENT UPSTAIRS
99	THE BONE KEEPER
100	YOU'RE DEAD TO ME
101	DESECRATION
102	I KNOW YOU, TOO
103	SIT PRETTY
104	HAVE YOUR MUSE, I'LL HAVE MY WHISKEY
105	THE NEXT BIG THING
106	PANDERING
107	I WANT TO BURN
108	GAMBLING WITH SOULS
109	STILL, HERE
110	SHE, OF THE DARKEST
111	SOMEONE ELSE'S WAR
112	TWENTY EIGHTEEN
113	DESIRE
114	MUSE ME OR USE ME
115	CHASING TWILIGHT
116	AGAIN, DARLING
117	INKED

118   THE HARD PART OF THE NIGHT

119   A SLOW LEAK

120   MY HEART BREAKING TOMORROW

121   IN STATIC AND STEREO

122   IN THE END

123   REGRET

124   TURNING GOODBYE

125   WHEN IT RAINS

126   YES, I REMEMBER YOU

127   FUCKING HEARTS

128   CRACKLE AND HUM

129   THREE SHEETS TO FOREVER

130   A LONGEST WINTER

131   COLLECTING NOTHING

132   THE CURVE OF HER WISH

133   LIKE NEW

134   MIDNIGHT CRAVINGS

135   WIPING YOUR LIGHT

136   THE OUTSIDE DOESN'T MATCH THE IN

137   WHAT I MEANT TO SAY

138   IT NEVER HEARD THAT

141   I DEVELOPED A TASTE FOR IT

143   SYLLABLE BY SYLLABLE

144   DRAGON SOUL

145   LOVE BITES

This was my journey.
This was my pain.
This is my healing.

You have my heart.
You have my heart
here, I have left it
on these pages.

NOT ENTIRELY BROKEN, NEVER QUITE WHOLE

I am a lover of words
and tragically beautiful things,
poor timing and longing,
and all things with soul,
and I wonder if that means
I am entirely broken,
or if those are the things
that have been keeping me whole.

IN ALL THAT I AM

If I could draw a blade across my wrist to show you
that my veins clog with the sludge of ugliness,
you would never again ask me,
"Why are you so tired?"
If I could crack open my skull to free my mind,
you would see that it is not splintered by madness
but rather patched together with clarity,
you would never again ask me to swallow poison.
If I could rip this body open to show you
the raw red wounds that have been lashed
onto my soul by every inhumane atrocity
this world has endured,
you would never again ask me,
"Why are you so sad?"
Instead, your accusing eyes demand simple words
to simpler questions that the simplest minds
can process, and in all that I am, simple I am not.

THE DRAW

Some souls
were never meant
to be content.

MY DAYS ARE NUMBERED

My moods have been predetermined and prescribed.
Seven tiny compartments measure my days.
Pink and orange match the sunrise
and taste bitter with my coffee.
I chase them with water so they
mellow in my blood,
as if water can render toxic harmless.
Yellow sticks in my throat every morning,
and steals my happiness before it can shine.
White dissolves under my tongue,
it can't get in fast enough,
the impatient little fucker.
If white is late, I start to itch.
Blue makes me saddest of all.
Without blue, the rest is just candy,
and I will never sleep again.
I'm always packing a rainbow wherever I go.

A DEVIL AND A DEITY

There is a beast
in me who quakes
to be worshipped.
Its deep rumbling
cracks the temple
of me and I wait
to crumble beneath it.

IMPETUS

The tide
has pulled
the storm
from my soul,
again.

BLOOD MOON

Call me down.
I have squeezed
blood from the moon
and taken all I can
and still, she smiles,
and I have yet
to find the light
that used to be mine.

THEY TAKE ME UNDER, SOMETIMES

I have never seen battles
quite as terrifyingly beautiful
as the ones I fight
when my mind splinters
and races, to swallow me
into my own madness, again.

OF MANIACS AND MANICS

You understand words like,
empty, dry, and **nothing**
but you'll never know
what hollow feels like
because your mind
will never take you under.
It won't swallow the smile
from your daughter's face
before it ever reaches your eyes.
You understand words like,
full, vibrant, and **ecstasy**
but you'll never know
what euphoria feels like
when you walk, body hot
on a wet summer's day
into a cool room,
worlds colliding on your skin.
You call me crazy
because I feel everything,
but I feel sorry for you
because you don't.

SOMETHING PURE

I am tired and I just want
something pure, something
beautiful to burst
from the filth of this sickness,
this tragedy that is
devouring my mind again.
And all at once I feel
nothing but the shriek
of my soul being
ripped from its bones.

FREIGHT TRAINS

My life can be boiled down
to nothing more than
a series of tracks hauling
freight trains filled with intensity,
and me, the ultimate train wreck,
just itching to play chicken.

AN EARWORM IN A GHOST

I am heavy with the weight of the world,
a ghost of the girl I used to be.
Where is she, the one with the feet
that skimmed the ground?
I can hear her still, deep within
the walls of my mind, drumming
her knuckles to the beat of dying
dopamine; oh, how it wails over
the strumming of her airy melody.

STEALING BREATH

There are lost souls
wandering,
stealing breath
to be the ones,
who breathe
life back in.
And sometimes,
I find myself
walking among them.

DEPRESSION SLEEPS

Tonight I will sleep.
I will sleep away
the sadness,
and when I wake
I hope to find
I did not sleep
my entire life away.

ANOTHER SEASON

The shadows are making their way
to my door again, and my stoop
has been painted in grey,
but I know that soon the grey
will give way to the blackness
and I will spend another season
crushing bricks and sprinkling salt
in every corner of my fragile mind.

THE LONG ROAD HOME

It's been a while since I've walked this
dusty road, but I remember it well.
That spot there, where the sun
never quite reaches, is where
I found myself on my knees praying
to a god, I didn't believe in.
Bodies upon bottles
upon razor blades gleaming
with self-harm and a cocaine glow
fill the ditches beside me,
and the trenches of my memories.
In this place the hills are alive
with the sound of sudden drops
and last gasps and the air is thick
with the stench of shame.
This is a long road, and east is west
and north is every failure I have ever eaten.
South lies, between humility and every lie
I have ever sworn in your blood.

MELANCHOLY

Melancholy, my longest
lost lover has returned,
to dance with me, again.

A COLLECTION OF MADNESS AND MAGIC

My mind is light and dark and always uneven,
a rest stop for a long line of weary travellers
and mischief makers; home to thousands
of manic spiders spinning sticky webs
of dark delusions against the back of my eyes.
My ears itch with the whispers
of hyper-charged bits of paranoia.
My throat burns from the speed
at which I swallow the rants
and raves of transient thoughts,
and I am able to breathe again.
My blood boils with electricity,
ferocious enlightenment kicking
through the walls of a dead heart
and I am alive again.
A collection of madness and magic,
I am a place where art and illness collide.

MIDNIGHT MIND

It's midnight in my mind again;
my thoughts are burning
and bursting like shooting stars.
Every breath is a bullet exploding
behind my eyes and dropping
bits of wishes down the back
of my neck, to die, and dying itches,
between my shoulder blades,
in that spot, I can never quite reach.

MY MANIC MIND

Imagine if you will, the fair has come to town. Take in all of the sights and sounds, from the toddlers crying to the pre-teens laughing. They're running and trying to cut in line at the ride that promises the biggest thrill. You smell the deep-fried doughnuts, french fries and cotton candy. You hear the carnies yell out, "Bet you can't make this shot, three for a dollar, step right up." Every sound is amplified, from the creaks of the rusted gears on the Ferris wheel to the poor kid who is puking behind the fortune teller's trailer. Everything is ALIVE. You look right and then left, which way do you go? It's a maze of debauchery and adrenaline.

Chaos and pleasure are hidden around every corner. You want it all, but where do you start? You have only purchased enough tickets to ride two times, which will you choose? Do you spend your tickets in the funhouse, reflecting on your reflections? This one is too small. This one is too big. This one is just right, and it's as creepy as sin. You've seen your soul in the mirror at a circus, and it scares the hell out of you. Move on. Something has to take the sting away. One ticket left. You clutch it as if it were your payment to the boatman on the River Styx. Anxiety starts to swell. The noise is becoming too much and something inside of you has built up, you don't understand what it is, all you know is that it needs to be released.

All you can focus on is the feeling that you must get out of you. There is no talking this down; there is only a primal instinct to shred every sense of dignity you thought you had.

The noise and the lights beckon you to stay, join us, and partake in this pleasure. Lose yourself in the rush. Forget all of your worries and everything that ties you down and just fucking LIVE. Take the feelings inside of you as far as you possibly can before you burst and shatter into thousands of unfulfilled dreams and promises. Find your release, and find it fast, they are closing the gates in mere minutes.

You follow the nervous screams and maniacal laughter until you see it, the main attraction. The rollercoaster is boasted as being the fastest and scariest ride to come to town. You trip trying to make your way to it as fast as you can. All pleasantries are off. You'll push small children out of your way because you know what that rush feels like. You've turned into a junkie now; you need the escape. The release.

As you make your way to your seat, you push past the people that refuse to ride in the front. What's the point if you can't stare into the abyss on your rapid cycle back to the ground? You buckle yourself in, front row seats, but not too tight though, the rush of potential death gets you off. The attendant comes by to make sure you're secure. You fight the urge to spit in his face and tell him to fuck off.

You're pissed off at the time it takes for every other sucker to get belted in. This is your ride, and they have neither clue nor any business being on it. You run this coaster, and it moves when you say so. The climb up the tracks feels like a sad sort of foreplay to you. You hear the gears churn and the squeals of the unimportant people who've hitched a ride behind you. When the coaster reaches the peak, it stops, and your heart starts to pound. You are so out of sync with everyone here but in tune with everything that matters. For the briefest of moments, you are free. The air is thinner, and there is nothing above you but sky and possibilities. If you unhooked your seat belt right now you know for certain that you could fly.

You raise your face to the heavens and take a deep breath; the anticipation of the plunge is ecstatic. Raise your arms and feel your ass lift off the seat. Like lightning, the coaster dives into its descent. The speed is finally a match for all of the thoughts that race through your mind; it overtakes and for a second there is stillness. The quiet ecstasy of something that is more powerful than you, and it is delectable. You've met your match, and you urge it on, faster, harder, DO NOT STOP.

The coaster whips and weaves over its tired and worn track. People scream and even cry, begging for it to stop. You shut them out while focusing on the way the wind howls through your hair. The impulse to keep riding swells to a radiant compulsion. Before it is half over, you are devising a way to get more tickets. You can't even be satisfied with the thrill of the ride. All you can think about is how you will be able to make it possible to ride again, and again, and again...

You are finally free. There is something more powerful than you, and the innate instinct to harness all of it overtakes every sense you have. You are no longer here to release anything. You are here to devour and discard until you finally feel full.

There is no end to this fair, this ride, and this hunger; there is only that swift descent into oblivion.

A POCKET FULL OF MANIA

I have sidled up to demons
and whispered them to sleep
but these fiery angels
in my pocket care nothing
for decent conversation.

FAST AND FEROCIOUS

I was meant to burn,
fast and ferocious,
like a comet,
and you were meant
to watch me burn out.
Scrambling to catch
my sparks before they were gone.

A FURIOUS ASCENSION

She watched stiff-backed girls
in snow-white paper dresses flying,
their speckled kites
low to the ground, and she called
for the great gusts of angry winds
to blow in and catch the corners
of those dresses and kites,
and take them all, tangled together
into stormy places behind her eyes.
Sweep them into deep places
where held breath burns
against walls of lungs
before sighing into ecstasy.
Leave them in dark places where
terrified screams scorch the backs
of throats, and rip pain into pleasure.
Bury them among stark bones that found
their lustre in the depths of her mind.

BENEATH DARKNESS

We were not made of star stuff.
Perhaps the ash ground beneath
Lucifer's boot is where we were born.

EERIE ALONES AND JAMS OF TRAFFIC

It's an eerie kind of alone
when your world comes
crashing down
and you're on your knees
with nothing
but agony for company.
When everything is spinning
out of control
and you are powerless
to get back what is gone,
clarity hits hard.
How strange it is,
when a life shatters,
the sun still rises;
traffic still jams,
and people carry on.
It's an odd feeling
to scream into nothing
and ask for a pause
just for one second,
to catch a breath,
because life should stop
for a moment,
at that moment
when your world
has fallen apart,
just so you can
catch your breath.

SHADES OF NEVER ENOUGH

I bleed truth
and trying
to please you,
but all you see
are the shades
of never enough,
dripping from the pen
that you gave to me.

WHEN MY SHADOW SPEAKS

You demand my pretty
words on happy days
to mend your broken heart,
but when the sun hits my back
and my shadow speaks
its truth, you cower
in horrified judgment.
You say you want
to know my soul
but the truth is that
my light would blind you
long before you could
ever drown in my darkness.

I HAVE SURRENDERED ON THIS NIGHT

Tonight, I will unpack my worries,
tuck them gingerly beneath my pillow,
and lay my head upon them
so that they may feel safe.
When I close my eyes against
the violence of racing thoughts,
perhaps they shall see the red
streaking the white of them and
know I have surrendered on this night.
As I sink down into the darkness,
strength drifts out and away
from me to take first watch at my feet.

ANCHORED

Until you have tethered
your madness
to someone else's sanity
in order to keep breathing,
you don't know vulnerability.

THIS SIDE OF MIDNIGHT

I believe there is a window mounted in mourning
and hung from sharp corners, just this side
of midnight, and when we call out through
its shattered glass and send our deepest wishes
through its torn screens, something in the universe
shifts to allow our darkest echoes
and our most unfortunate words to ride
the wind and carry our secrets into the open
windows of all the lonely insomniacs of the world;
the tragic beasts who spend their nights walking
with demons and wrestling with their mental health
while they wish they weren't wishing this world away.
And I think if we whisper just a little bit louder
than library vibes, and a pitch higher than the purists
that preach Monday love on Sunday Mornings,
we could spill our secrets before the clock strikes done,
and maybe someone who has spent their night
wandering can find a place to rest their feet
and open a window on their side of midnight
to breathe deep the voices that never took
the time to walk them home at dawn.

I SEE YOU

I see you grinding another day,
battered and exhausted refusing to stop.
I see your fists, swollen and split
knuckled; dripping with the quit
you beat to the ground.
I see your tired eyes, bloodshot
from blinking against the grains
of you'll never be enough, swirling
sandstorms across your vision.
I see you, beat down and getting back up.
I see you, the fight in you,
and it is ferocious.
I see you, the heart of you,
and it is breathtaking.
I see you, the soul of you,
and it is magnificent.
I see you, all of you,
and you are fucking beautiful.

MESSY SHINE

I like dirty hearts
and restless minds,
the old souls that
have known hard lives;
the ones who cast
the most beautiful shine.

FROM STEADY SHORES

Oh my darling, you have eaten
far too many shadows
to ever believe that you have
spent even one day hiding.
A lighthouse can never see
the brilliance of its own light
guiding lost souls home.
It stands tall in the darkness,
steady, a beacon
for the hands that reach
and pull bodies to safety.
You are a lighthouse.
And they do push you
down to pull themselves
up, but you are steel
and blossom and bone,
and when lighting does strike,
the burst of your own radiance
will be so great that you
will finally understand
your own thunder.

SHE IS A STORM

Gently now, wild one.
This world can only handle
so many storms,
and you have struck this one
with your lightning
and painted the walls of it
with your thunder.
Gently now, wild one.
Let them catch their breath.

SHE WAS

She was reckless
and apprehensive.
She was cruel
and she was kind.
She was a beautiful
contradiction, living
large and dying inside.

O NEGATIVE

She was beautiful;
all thorns
and no roses,
but he didn't
mind bleeding.

FEEDING TIME

I know she is beautiful;
all hot breath and pretty words,
but she has starved her demons
for a lifetime now, and those
motherfuckers are hungry.

PERCUSSION

I never meant
to ruin him,
but I do love
the way his heart
still beats my name.

THE COSMOS ARE IN A GODDESS

She has stars in her eyes
and poetry on her lips,
and loving a girl like her
will bring you to your knees.

CALL ME A GODDESS AGAIN

You could ruin Heaven
for me, the way you
keep worshipping my name.

MIXED WITH A HINT

It was my words that spilled
from his lips,
my poetry that poured
from his soul;
how was I to resist
my own passion?
Mixed with a hint
of his own.

LONGING

Longing, my most
shameless of lost lovers
has returned to cross
the oceans in my eyes
and stake temptation
as his claim.

UNDER RED SKIES

That night we smoked cigarettes
and talked of the red skies
that hung over us, above
right shoulders just East of town.
And although it was winter
and chaos danced
with the blowing snow,
I felt the heat of those red skies.
It was somewhere inside of forty-five
mile an hour winds and the second
bottle of wine where I fell in love.

ON THE HIPS OF A HURRICANE

I could love you less
than storms or anything
easy that I have ever done,
but you, my hard love,
I love you as the moon
loves the tides, pulling
and pushing for one minute
only, for you to see that this life,
that our life, could be extraordinary
on the hips of a hurricane or riding
the shoulders of a tropical storm.
You and I could devastate worlds,
the way we love each other,
churning and bursting inside
winds that will never kiss our lips.
You are my disaster,
and I will wait forever for you
to decide to ravage my shores.

STAR SONGS AND MOONLIGHT

You are my
deepest wishes,
a dark summer
sun blazing
sweet secrets
onto bronzed hips.
You are star
songs and moonlight
kisses I hide
under my shirt.

STICKY SOUR DANCING

Let us turn on the lights
and take off this skin we are in.
The only thing to come
between our shadows
shall be our bones.
I like the way the light catches
our vulnerability, quivering
in the beds of old fractures.
And the smell of our marrow mixing,
sticky sour dancing under my nose,
wets my tongue, and spills my secrets
through barren valleys, split
between the grooves beneath my hips.

BUT YOU WERE

Not all prisons
have locks
not all secrets
are sacred
but you
were
midnight whispers
trapped inside
twisted minds
and heavy hearts.

ILLUSIONS OF LOVE

Sometimes love is nothing
more than a sticky web;
illusions spun
from clever minds
and bitter hearts.

NEITHER HEAVEN NOR HELL

He calms my chaos
and I fuel his fire.
We are a match made
between Heaven and Hell.

I SHOULD HAVE KNOWN BETTER

He had the smile of an angel
and the mind of a devil,
and I should have known better.
But he planted flowers in my heart
and made hell feel like home.

SOMETHING ACHINGLY BEAUTIFUL

Love was never easy
because suffering was
never optional.
But there was something
gorgeous in the act
of arching backs writhing
in anticipation of ripping
hearts from chests,
something achingly beautiful
in the brutality of it all.

JUNK

He was intense, a drug,
and I couldn't get enough,
no matter how much
of him I consumed.
He was potent and powerful
and he ruined me,
and I yearned to ruin.
I kept going back for more.
I swear if I were to rip myself open,
it wouldn't be blood that poured
out of me, it would be him.

HEAVY HANDS

I used to wonder how
I could love him;
but he crept in slowly,
inch by careful inch
until he no longer reeked
of her and the kids he never
really wanted anyway.
But his hands grew heavy
until they left hints of him behind,
and I became the one who reeked
of dirty things and wondered
how anyone could ever love me.

PEACE BY PIECE

It's during the moments when I'm quiet
that I foolishly give in to the idea of peace,
I should know better by now.
With every blow you laid on me,
you stripped me of any chance of peace
that I could have hoped for.
Now the bruises have healed,
the scars blended into shades of me,
faded into almost gone... almost.
The almost is what kills me again,
taunts me and tells me what a coward I was.
It's the almost, the faded pieces
that bring up everything I never did,
every single thing I never said.
Unspoken fears rise up and curdle
against my tongue and they threaten
to choke me, so I swallow them again,
every last word I never said to you,
and the burn explodes through my body,
shredding it piece by piece, promising
a life without peace, if they go unsaid once more.

THE NIGHT A BLUE MOON BURST

The sun has set a thousand times
since the night a blue moon burst
and I opened my door to a wolf
grinning wildly, chewing on my name.
My, what spectacular eyes he had;
deep pools of golden madness
churning the reflection of my surprise
into blazing fire that broke his gaze
and seared fear into my flesh.
My pulse raced, leaping to ride
the sweet stench of terror ripping
holes through my veins before it danced
under the great weight of his paws
crushing the walls of my chest.
The sun has set a thousand times
since the night a blue moon burst,
and cast its shadow upon pebbles,
and the wolf that would steal my breath.
But even now, on the eve of a rising
I can barely breathe until I hear them
howling in the distance,
and then I will drift,
pulling wilderness from my hair
under the light of a quiet moon.

EVANESCENCE

I swear I was clean before
you came blazing in,
guns firing hot, bursting
into me with pain so sweet
that I begged for a slow death.
But you stole the sweet ache
from my bones and left
the savage bits of you behind,
spraying them all over my world.
They blot out the sun, and
leave me with a forever night.
They crawl over me, inside of me,
and consume me with the filth
of memories, and they whisper
about this slow death and how
I should be careful what I wish for.

THE COLOUR OF US

Water is wet and grass is green
and we are us, until it isn't
and we aren't, anymore.
And that's how it was, he and I,
right from the start: peas and carrots,
sand and surf, heaven and hell.
We were the late night phone calls
that went straight to voicemail,
the last light in the window
when all other doors were locked.
We were voracious laughter
muffling horrified screams.
We were bodies twisted in ecstasy
and minds broken in angst.
We were psych stays and breakdowns,
pills popped and death threats,
sirens wailing and holding cells.
We were life, on a September morning,
and death on an April night,
and in our own minds we were golden.

A COSMIC DISAPPOINTMENT

I drink
and I scream
and I curse the stars,
and still you are here,
blaring in my fucking veins.

SINISTER LOVERS

I have come to believe that death
and insomnia are the most sinister lovers,
for it is only at three a.m. when I am restless
that my body aches with phantom pains
and your ghost returns to torment my mind.

TOMB GRAZING

Every now and then
I roam the catacombs
in my head and attempt
to resurrect you, and
make you shiny again.

THE SILENCE OF YOU

Even now, when
the wind whispers
your name
across my skin,
the silence of you
is deafening.

LITTLE DEATHS

There are little deaths
in every bit of remembering,
and all of the forgetting.
The truth is I don't know
if I should bleed for you,
or for me.

TASTING PAIN

I loved him, intensely.
Throat bared, holes in the walls,
sirens wailing, intensely.
But God, did I love him.
I knew we would end
before we had even begun.
But my name was blackened
on his chest and confessions
had been whispered at three a.m.
and I couldn't breathe without him.
And until you have tasted pain
as sweet as his, you can't
begin to understand.

FUCK YOU, DARLING

Forgive me, darling.
I still struggle
to put you into words;
how ridiculously arrogant of me.
To think I could ever hope
to grace this world
with your light when all I have
to give is empty lines
and a devastated heart.
Fuck you, darling, for taking
my soul when you left.

TO NOTHING

How recklessly
we turn
from strangers
to lovers,
and blindly back
to nothing.

MY EASY HEART

I have always loved the cold
dark places where feelings go
to hide, as I have loved something
about the easy way my heart
shatters the second it rubs
up against something warm.

CAN'T HAVE IT ALL

I need you
to look me in the eyes
and go to battle
with the demons
that lurk
and look back
at you, and then
I need you
to love us back
into redemption.

GLEAMING BONES

I would shed my skin
to gleam bones for you,
in every way you would
never dare ask.
And that, my want
to bare souls while
others skim pretty, is
the only gift I have that is
worthy enough, to give to you.

THE OFFERING

I bled out and into him,
for him, every time he asked.
And he asked, and I withered
while I bled and he watched.

SACRIFICE

You load your words
as I bare my chest,
and this will be
the most beautiful death.

JUST YOU WAIT

Be patient, pretty
little tragic one,
the real suffering
has not yet begun.

LITTLE BLACK DRESS

Oh, how she walks.
Draped in demons,
dripping despair,
she is the prettiest hell.

I ONCE WAS NEW

My body has been used;
tossed to the ground
to wipe away indiscretions,
and the grinding filth
of lying whores.

My heart has been starved;
cupped in sweaty palms
to ease burdens,
and the murky hypocrisy
of righteous men.

My spirit has been wrung;
pulled inside of fists
to stretch truths,
and the sour hesitation
of bitter regret.

My soul has been worn;
placed upon rails
to catch tears,
and the heavy wetness
of desperate sins.

I COULD ALMOST SPARKLE

The truth is I liked the filth of it all.
I was a fucking mess,
but eventually life demanded
cleanliness, and eventually
I could almost sparkle.
Still every now and again I'll slip,
and cast my shadow to the delight
of the other sparkling messes
afraid of their own.
They cool their heels
and laugh, patting each other
on the backs for shining
so bright that their tiny things
will grow dull. I watch them
from my shadow, wrapped
in the warmth of my cleanest
tiny things that will grow wild
and bright despite the mess of me,
and in that moment,
when their lights fade
and the breeze meets the sweat
on the back of my neck,
in that moment I am clean.

DISCHARGED

It was addicting, the attempt
to lose myself inside
all the others, until
I chilled my bones
in the shadows cast by stoic
backs and upturned eyes
that refused to see me, sacrificing.

I WAS HERE

I will not tread lightly.
I want you to know,
by the quake in your bones
and the falter of your step,
that I was here before you,
and I fought valiantly.

LOVE HAS NEVER

Love has never asked to be felt;
it has never once bowed its head
to kiss my palms or ask me
what it would take to make
room for it in my soul.
Love has never spent a moment
gathering my dreams or getting
to know me a little bit better;
it never once offered to scrub
the stains your broken heart left
in the corners of my soul.
Love has laughed in the face
of my consent, demanded
a place at my table,
and shoved its filthy hands
down my throat, and it pulls
my heart from its cage
and the words from my mouth
and stacks them like secrets
inside your hooded eyes
and perfect lines until I look
less like me and more like
a casualty of poor choices
and cheap moments spent
in gaudy rooms shooting
the shit and anything that feels
a little like love into my veins.

STOIC

I will not force
a pretty smile
upon my face
to please eyes
that no longer
see me.

BURSTING PURE AND BLOOMING

Landlocked and scraping my belly
in the depths of their apologies,
I learned to hold my breath
in an ocean of abandonment.
The bitter taste of sunny days
danced upon my tongue,
twisting with the weeds
of their neglect before
I swallowed them,
and felt the tear of my lungs
bursting pure, and blooming
the greenest words from my throat.
The feathered stroking
of doubtful creatures making homes
out of the shame in my veins
screamed for release, and oh
how I released them, into deaf ears
and cruel eyes my soul flowed,
spilling truth and pouring pain,
into the deep pools of their shallow love.

HUSH

If I could claw the words
out of the back of my throat
and give them, dripping
of me, to you, we would
talk of sticky hands,
and the messes they make.

THAT DAY, AT DINNER

The day she chose to strip herself
of everyone else's opinions
was the first time she knew strength,
held courage, and felt beauty.
That was the day when she finally
understood what it meant to be free.

GUTTING THE APARTMENT UPSTAIRS

From time to time,
the sun will set hot
on my memories
and leave the cooling
to a breeze that swings
by my house and kicks
my front door down
just to tickle my lips
and call us square,
but I bite my lip
when I stand in line,
self-serving at a checkout,
juggling multiple screws
and my home improvement,
and always wondering
if I should go back
and thumb through
the racks of red
swatches named so sweetly
as 'cherry', 'blush', and 'love',
by someone who has never
tasted passion, or love, or us,
or the way I thought love should
taste when it rolled
off of your tongue and poured
into my mouth before
I inhaled my smirk
and swallowed
the lies of everyone here
who has lined up before me.

THE BONE KEEPER

I have cleaned my closet of all of the bones
to make room for wispy summer dresses.
I wrapped those bones in shame
and tucked them deep into bags of guilt.
With the strings of regret, I tied the bags
closed and knotted them with resentment.
I lifted the bags one by one, the weight
of their bitterness trying to crush me,
and I carried them to the spot
where the bend finally breaks.
I dug deep to pull strength to shred earth,
and I dug; past coffins and fossils
and I didn't stop until I hit never again.
My twisted arms were mighty
when I pulled myself out of that pit,
and as I stood and exhaled gratitude,
I let the bags fall into the abyss,
no longer the keeper of your bones.

YOU'RE DEAD TO ME

And now I shall bury you,
remembering you as if
you had only been seasons.

DESECRATION

I found the pieces
you tried to hide,
buried in secret
places, untouched.
Oh, how I yearn
to lash the beauty
of them and leave
my stain upon each one.

I KNOW YOU, TOO

I know you know me.
By the ache
in your bones
and the pulse
in your veins,
you know me,
and God help you,
I know you too.

SIT PRETTY

I want to be cruel.
I want to lash out at everyone
who has used me,
and I want to do it over
and over again.
I want them all to know
what ungrateful feels like.
I want them
to wear the cloak of unloved,
slip into taken for granted,
and sit pretty in thankless.
I want them to feel
what it is like to be sliced
open so the vampires can feed.
I want them to give and give
and give until they have nothing
left to give, and then
I want them to give some more.
And then maybe, just maybe
they will understand.

HAVE YOUR MUSE, I'LL HAVE MY WHISKEY

Write your poetry and chew
the words that curdle
in your mouth or spit
them at me, I want
to know how it feels to
slide down my own face.
Am I still pretty
in the back of your throat?
No, you prefer me
streaking down my chin,
all narcissistic and gooey
mingling with the love
things you hate so much.
Spit me out, and step on me.
I will stick to the bottom
of your shoe and perhaps
you can look away
when you scrape your sole
against the edge of the curb
outside your bedroom window,
and when I dry up in the night.
I was pretty there,
in the back of your throat,
and you could have made
a home beneath my fingernails.

THE NEXT BIG THING

And you, with your twenty-year-old,
come-hither-face, shimmering
with the light of the sun,
and a life that has yet to be lived.
Look at you, unmarked and perfect,
recycling the pretty words
that you have eaten, and
the lovely ideas of all the tragedies
that you have never even tasted.
I don't like the way you keep
trying to force them down my throat,
as if choking on your nothing
could possibly cleanse me
of the suffering I have swallowed.
Darling, I see you,
all twenty years of you,
and I will invite you to my table,
set the prettiest place for you
to come back to me,
after you have gagged on life,
wiped your mouth,
and asked for a second fucking helping.

PANDERING

Sometimes I feel as if
I am pandering to savages,
sealing my soul and selling it
for an innocent kiss
or a quick fix.
And then I push and I shove,
and I make my way
to the front of the line
to buy it all back
from the wasted souls
who look an awful lot like me.

I WANT TO BURN

I wish you could
feel what I feel,
the intensity of it all,
and how it is
almost too much
but never quite enough.
The warmth
in the darkness
the chill
of the light,
and all the ways
I want to burn.

GAMBLING WITH SOULS

Some of us sell pretty
versions of our ugly
selves and call it truth;
others fold our pretty
truths into ugly lies
and call it even.
We are illusionists,
realists, the gamblers
of souls, and we all pay
the poet, in the end.

STILL, HERE

They have turned
their backs
but I am still here.
I am still,
here.

SHE, OF THE DARKEST

She is of the strangest beauty
and the darkest courage.
and when she walks
with intent the earth
trembles beneath her feet.

SOMEONE ELSE'S WAR

I have been caught in
the palm of crooked hands,
slid myself along promises
down pinky fingers
and into the throats
of corrupt bedfellows.
My mouth tastes of shame
but my eyes glisten
with the spoils
of someone else's war.

TWENTY EIGHTEEN

I want to love harder and hotter
than I ever have before,
and I want it to bend me in passion
until winter breaks into spring.
I want to find inspiration along roads
I have never thought to travel,
and I want to feel peace
in the waters I have never waded in.
I want to feel the pulse of cities
I have never set foot in,
and hear the stories of strangers
on a Wednesday afternoon.
I want to see beauty in eyes
that have never looked into mine,
and smell the colour
green on a rainforest floor.
I want to run faster than
my body has ever had to run,
and catch spring as she is winking
her way into summer.
I want to carry love in my hands
until they are overflowing
and place it in the hearts
I have broken before.
I want to climb until I can climb
no higher, and feel summer
give way and surrender to fall.
I want to hear laughter and love
mixed with leaves crunching,
and I want to light fires
in our hearts to warm our winter souls.

DESIRE

Desire, my hungriest
lost lover has returned
to consume me.
To set fire to my blood
and stroke his cravings
through my soul.

MUSE ME OR USE ME

Muse me, angel baby.
Ink me into bluish greys
and drop me in splashes.
Let me run, and drip
down creamy pages.

CHASING TWILIGHT

We went to bed in the cruellest places,
hoping to wake to beautiful things.
And I suppose the way twilight crept
through gauzy drapes and cracked glass
to lay its cool glow over sleepy eyes,
held a particular kind of beauty.
For when dawn crawled through
torn drapes and shattered glass
to lay its tired glow over wounded eyes,
we yearned to chase twilight
into the cruellest places, again.

AGAIN, DARLING

I have torn my wings
again, darling
and the blisters are raw
on my feet,
but I will meet you deep
in the woods with nothing
more than a cold heart
and a fiery soul.
I have been watching clocks
again, darling
and how flowers bloom
the way seasons die,
and I have been waiting for you.

INKED

I carved you deep.
Your words on my mind,
your name into my skin.

THE HARD PART OF THE NIGHT

You left me to hold the hard parts
of our life and the night, and I still
try to mute the sound of my own heart
breaking, but it breaks again and again,
over and over until the shards of it
climb from my chest and pull my lungs
from my throat, my lungs that have been
blackened with the thickest part
of the night and I am left choking.
I cough and I spit blood, and I hide
my words inside the grooves
of pointy molars before they crumble
and end up beneath my tongue.
I remember when my mouth was full
of gleaming promises before
I pushed my own fingers down my throat
and treated the burn of it all
with whiskey neat and love gone bad.
I remember what it felt like to smile
before my smile met your fist
and I grew ignorant when I spat
my wisdom and your name
into our kitchen sink.
And now moving on has become
the thing that looks sweeter
this year, but my lost socks,
and your sweet lies leave
a film on every tack in the wall
that once held our memories
and the to-do lists we never got around to.
But they still look pretty
on a cork board that hints

you once loved me, and maybe
I loved you, but I still slur
my words and hide your lies
underneath my lost truth.

A SLOW LEAK

Little
by little,
drop
by drop,
everything
fades away.

MY HEART BREAKING TOMORROW

Today my lips are chapped
from all of the kisses I have
given away, and I can already
feel my heart breaking
again tomorrow.
I have set my soul to repeat
every yesterday when
the vision I held of myself
was still as clear and half
as clean as the hope
I watched you bury
in the earth that smelled
faintly as fresh as my mother
when she used to tell me
how much she loved me
as she scrubbed my hair.
We would laugh when
the strands found their way
beneath her nails
and see-sawed the day away
and her hands clean again.
I smiled when I watched her
pound our garden and her love
into dinner with hands cleaner
than they had any right to be,
and here I am now, pounding
love into supper and scratching
desolate grounds open, and I
watch you bury the leftovers
while I pray for spring rains
to fall and wash it all away,
even though nothing will
ever grow in this place.

IN STATIC AND STEREO

Leave her to the corners
of her mind and the radio.
She will heal inside
sad songs and memories.

IN THE END

I have known love
and I have known loss,
but in the end,
they both looked
a lot like you.

REGRET

Regret, my wistful
lost lover has returned
to torment me, churning
riptides through my veins
to breach my heartbreak
and flood his madness into my soul.

TURNING GOODBYE

It was colder than usual that morning,
the way the wind was blowing just so,
I heard the sun weeping her love,
into the moon and its fading glow.
And I watched the stars as they flickered
to the beat of my broken heart,
as if someone was dancing across them
turning goodbye into a work of art.

WHEN IT RAINS

I can still feel you inside of me,
the pieces you left behind,
embedded into my bones,
and they ache when it rains
and when I almost forget
that you're gone.

YES, I REMEMBER YOU

Yes, I remember you.
I remember the hitch
and the gasp before
my veins opened up
into fields upon fields
upon barren wastelands.
I remember how thunder felt
that night when a thousand
wild stallions carried my pulse
around the mountains of my bones
and placed it where I hoped
I would never remember you again.

FUCKING HEARTS

Every fucking night
I wrestle the pieces
of my heart back out
of your bloody hands,
and then I wake, bleeding
from my chest and I spend
my day wondering why
the good girls always
make their beds inside
the bad boys' fucking hearts.

CRACKLE AND HUM

I will line them all up,
the many versions of me
you broke, and couldn't,
and tried to break again,
and I will whisper them stories,
tuck them in and talk of tall
tales of you and me and love,
and all manner of make-believe.
They will know of the happy
endings that never came,
the ones still waiting
in the rain outside the lines,
behind police tape, and inside
dial tones too weak to do anything
other than crackle and hum.

THREE SHEETS TO FOREVER

Not everyone drinks to forget.
Some of us wander, broken
and confused, trying to recall
that one perfect moment
before our worlds fell apart;
the moment when everything
lined up... stars, souls, magic...
some of us hold on long after
that moment was ripped away.
We all have our moments,
the ones that could convince us
to give up everything
just to go back and relive
one second one more time.
No, we don't all drink to forget,
some of us drink to remember.

A LONGEST WINTER

There is something here still,
something you left behind,
and it is bitter like winter
and I am aching for spring.

COLLECTING NOTHING

I waste time wishing
I could go back and collect
wasted moments spent waiting
for something that never came,
or ended too fast,
or just wasn't enough.
And the absurdity of it all,
wasting time over wasted time,
collecting nothing upon nothing
to fill a hole where nothing lives,
is the only way to assure that
nothing will leave me empty again.

THE CURVE OF HER WISH

Perception is a tricky thing.
Sometimes what she believes
to be real is nothing more
than the sound lonely wishes make
when she has wrapped them
in defeat and set them loose
into a thirsty world.
And in those moments,
when I am picking her up
off the floor again, I wipe her
eyes and tell her there is nothing
wrong with a love built for speed
and something poetic about a woman
built for broken hearts.

LIKE NEW

It all comes out
in the wash.
Get in the water,
my love, things
are never quite
as dirty as they seem.

MIDNIGHT CRAVINGS

I crave nothing in this life
like I crave forgiveness.
I practice rolling it around
my mouth, bouncing it off
my cheeks, and tucking it
beneath my tongue, just
incase I ever have a right to taste it.

WIPING YOUR LIGHT

There is something in you
I am unable to reach,
but I feel it, I feel you.
I feel your pain, and I see
your light spilling
from cupped palms placed
at the foot of unworthy altars.
And try as I might, I stretch
and I twist to reach you,
to empty your hands
of that brilliant pain,
but each time I twist
I come up empty-handed,
and wiping your light
from the corners of my mouth.

THE OUTSIDE DOESN'T MATCH THE IN

Look at these worlds
bursting inside my head,
these words burning
beneath my tongue.
Quickly, whisper me
your secrets and I will build
beauty from your pain as if
I was a craftsman, an artist,
something more than a lying fool.

WHAT I MEANT TO SAY

I don't remember the exact words
I said to you, but I do remember
how they tasted bitter
and unforgiving, and
what I really meant to say,
was that you were always lovely,
even as you were walking away.

IT NEVER HEARD THAT

I don't want to remember exactly
how I was or who I was before you,
and I know that isn't what this world
wants to hear, but it never listened
to the beat of my broken heart
or caught the pain in my eyes anyway.
It never heard the way I hated myself
when dawn hit my window and sliced
its way through the mountains of
maybe next time I won't hurt myself,
but for now, just cut these colours
easy enough to taste something
less bitter than I am, it never heard that.
It never listened to the way I could
gulp and howl under the light
of a full moon, a new moon, of any moon,
of a sick and sculpted summer moon
that hung above the grime I pretended
not to notice, it never heard that.
It never listened to my voice calling out
from the dark when the last light in me
had been dimmed, it never came to chase
the shadows or the monsters that waited
to lunge the second the lights went out.
It was never there to shine hope
into my darkened heart or hear the cries
of my soiled soul, it never heard that.
I never knew that silence with you whispered
the most extraordinary tales,
and sitting in the way of sunsets
with you shifted the ugly inside of me,
and burst beautiful rays into the dark of my eyes.

I don't want to remember
who I was when I was without you,
but I do, and I will, and perhaps
remembering how cold it was in the dark
will never let me forget how
I can hear the warmth in the light.

I DEVELOPED A TASTE FOR IT

I would have loved nothing more
back then to have left you gracefully,
but the match I had hidden
in my back pocket was yearning
to be struck as I had been
stricken with guilt and buried
underneath your lies somewhere
at the bottom of your soul,
next to the misfortune you carried
and scrawled into the words,
stained with every untruth
and tall tale you had written about me.
But in a perfect world, I would have
left them unread, and sealed
with something you loved
a little more than me,
but I am far from perfect,
and I have found that even at
my ugliest, when I was frothing
at the mouth and choking on your lies,
I developed a taste for it,
the sweet and sour ache
that comes with swallowing
air too heavy with excuse and
your kiss too chalky with pills.
I have taken a beat to dance
in rains hooked on chins
that droop with frowns full
of everything you say
you're going to do.
Those rains washed my soul clean
and those matches have burned

a hole in my pocket, perhaps I will
place them in my purse,
bury them under pens and trident,
next to old poems written
in pretty journals I have
kept just in case
life ever comes calling
and asks me to strike
my matches in your forest
and set your world on fire.

SYLLABLE BY SYLLABLE

And sometimes these words,
they save me, but sometimes,
most times, they kill me,
syllable by fucking syllable,
they rip me to shreds.

DRAGON SOUL

This life hasn't been easy on me,
I have learned to breathe fire,
and God help any of you who would
ever try to smother my flames.

LOVE BITES

I still pick at these
memories of you;
I pick them
until they bleed.

ACKNOWLEDGMENTS

As always I must give love and thanks to my publishing and editorial team, without Christine Ray and Kindra Austin, this book would have never made it out of our email chain. Thank you as always to my dear friend and wizard of all design, Mitch Green for taking my cover concepts and turning them into pure art, you are so badass.

To all of you who follow me on social media and take the time to comment and write heartfelt messages, I am a deep well of gratitude, one that will never run dry, it's because of all of you I have found my voice and my particularly peculiar shade of ink, and I thank you all for sticking with me.

Made in the USA
Lexington, KY
02 November 2019

56400424R00083